SuperQuick® Facebook – Easy and Fast Pages & Ads

Harness the Power of Facebook -
The Mysteries of Facebook, Fan/Business Pages, and FBML Revealed!

2d EDITION

By M. Nicole van Dam

To contact the Publisher:
SuperQuick® Publications, P.O. Box 583, Ojai, CA, 93024
Website: SuperQuick.bz   Email: SuperQuickBooks@aol.com

OTHER BOOKS BY M. NICOLE VAN DAM

SuperQuick ® Self-Publishing: On Demand Publishing & eBooks Made Easy

SuperQuick ® Savvy Business Thinking Points & Interviews

SuperQuick ® Facebook – Easy and Fast Pages & Ads – 2d Edn

SuperQuick® Wordpress – Easy, FREE and Fast Website, Smart Phone and e-Commerce Solutions!

SuperQuick® Solutions – Web Essentials: Time and Money Saving Tips for Website, Social Media and e-Commerce

Exploring the Successful You: A Guided Tour

Tempo – The Rhythm and Rhyme of the Artist

M. Nicole van Dam, a Retrospective 2010

Inca Dink, The Great Houndini

Rosie and Emma Plant a Seed

This Little Puppy

The Background Story of Inca Dink, The Great Houndini

*About the Cover Art: "Leap of Faith™" is a painting by M. Nicole van Dam.
To learn more, please visit* Nicole.bz

To see More Helpful Books from SuperQuick® Solutions, please visit SuperQuick.bz.
To see the author's artwork & Facebook presence, please visit Nicole.bz

Prelude

Why all this to-do about Facebook?

Answer: Facebook has a tremendous database (over **500,000,000** users and counting!) tailored so that you can target your ads to **exactly** your demographic.

Example: If you think your demographic is Cornell graduates who have dogs, you can choose to have your ad displayed to just Cornell grads that have dogs!

Facebook advertising is that powerful and easy to target!

That's why this effort is worth doing.

The way to use this book is to have it open on your lap while you work on Facebook on your computer – this book is a step-by-step guide.

Please come visit http://www.facebook.com/tinkerthethinker and see what the custom "Buried Bones" tab looks like before you like this page, and then like the page and see what you get!

This book is now one of Nicole's how-to series of books, published under the SuperQuick® brand. Each SuperQuick® book provides, so that others need not re-invent the wheel, a series of simple, hands-on steps to help other creatives and entrepreneurs achieve their goals. Re other M. Nicole van Dam SuperQuick® books: A great hands-on how-to book in this SuperQuick® series to get your started in pursuing your dreams is "SuperQuick® Success – Exploring the Successful You." If you're trying to get the right digital (internet, mobile and social media) presence for your business, brand, or creative endeavor, then SuperQuick® series has several hands-on how to books to help you: : "SuperQuick® Self Pubishing: On Demand Publishing & eBooks Made Easy," "SuperQuick® Facebook Pages & Ads," "SuperQuick® WordPress: Easy, FREE and Fast Website, Smart Phone and e-Commerce Solutions!" and "SuperQuick® Solutions – Web Essentials." Another handy guide in the SuperQuick® series is "SuperQuick® Savvy Business Thinking Points & Interviews," a thinking and talking points guide to ensure you enjoy the most fruitful conversation possible while networking with other entrepreneurs, investors, funders, consultants, and creatives, and to help you prepare for speaking engagements or moderate conferences and panels.

Table of Contents

Step 1

Create an Account at http://Facebook.com

Facebook first makes you set up a personal profile page BEFORE you can set up a page for your business. This is the easy part! All you need to do is go to Facebook.com and give sign up giving Facebook the information they request. When they ask you to import your contacts, I for myself skip that. My goal isn't to reach people who already know me, but to reach new people.

It's the way Facebook is – you need to set up a personal page before you can set up a business or fan page. –So even if you don't actually WANT a personal Facebook page, it's part of the drill.

For your career, to stand out, what you need to do, AFTER you create the bare bones basic personal page, is to create a second Facebook presence called a "Fan Page" or "Landing Page"

 This second Facebook presence (the "Fan Page" or "Landing Page", we will call it the "Fan Page") lets you customize the look of your Fan Page. If you hear the word FBML, don't be spooked – it stands for Facebook Markup Language, and in the real world,

5

FBML is a lot like HTML. If you already have a regular web page, the new Facebook (relative to the first edition I wrote of this book), let you import that entire URL into your new fan page, so you don't even need to know html type stuff anymore! Regardless, there are lots of wonderful free HTML resources on the web, so if you can do html, you can usually do FBML. Just know for now that in Facebookland they call their version of HTML by their own name - FBML (Facebook Markup Language).

Don't be confused: FBML and HTML are pretty much the same thing.

Step 2: Create Your Fan/Business Page

A. While you are in your new Facebook personal page, click on the "Home" button in the upper right corner of the top menu bar:

B. Click on "PAGES" in the left menu bar:

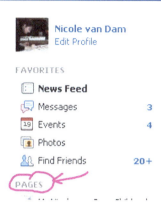

Nicole van Dam
Edit Profile

FAVORITES

News Feed

Messages   3

19 Events   4

Photos

Find Friends   20+

PAGES

C, Click on "Create a Page+"

D. In the resulting screen, pick the type of page you want to create – the choices are things like Business or Company or Brand or Artist, etc. Click on what fits your situation best and then fill in the information requested.

E. Facebook will guide you through a set-up process, asking for some basic about information, a profile picture (which you can simply upload from your computer), a Facebook web address (you may not get your first choice – I chose "TinkertheThinker" (which becomes facebook.com/tinkerthethinker) as I was writing this book simply because" Tinker" was taken. Facebook next asks you for a payment method – you can skip this. At the end of this process, you will see the Facebook admin panel for your new fan/business page – congratulations!

F. On the Facebook admin panel for your new fan/business page, you will see the profile picture you chose – if you click on it, you can edit it now or later. Click on Add a cover to create a large colorful banner on the top of your new fan page. Again, you can edit this at any time by clicking on it while you are in the Facebook admin panel.

G. Go down the screen – you will see little boxes that say "edit or remove" by when you joined facebook, etc – click it and choose to hide it as it will distract from your page.

Step 3: Creating a Custom Tab for Your Fan/Business Page

This step tells you how to make the COOL CUSTOM PART OF YOUR FAN PAGE:

A. Now comes the critical part: Look for the box that says photos, and click the down arrow next to it (see below for guidance):

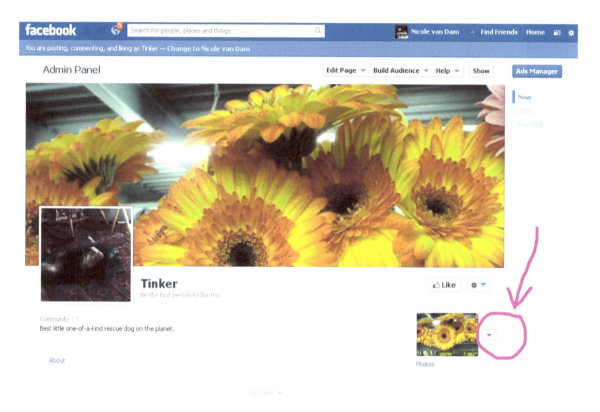

B. Type "static html" in the upper bar search box and hit enter – see below for guidance:

C. When you see the results, you will get a drop down box like the one below. Choose the one with the grey box and the star by clicking on it – see below for guidance:

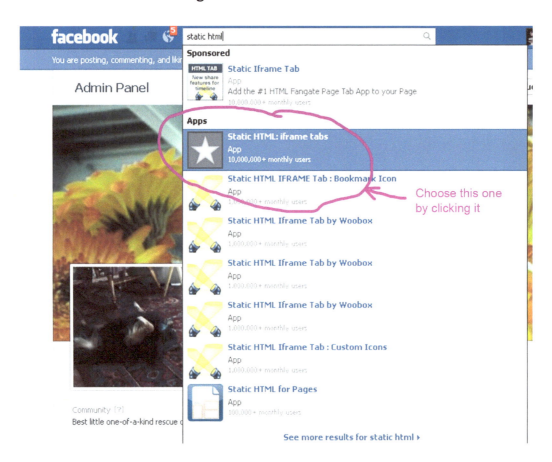

D. Next, click on the large blue box that says "Add Static HTML to a Page"

E. Next, use the deop down menu to choose the page you want to add the static html to – if this is your first fan page, you will only have one choice, but later as you progress you might do other pages as well. Click on your fan page to select it, and the screen will ask you to confirm by clicking on the blue box that says "Add Static HTML:iframe tabs" – click the blue box to confirm.

F. Your screen will now bring you back to your fanpage – but there is now a new item on it – see the grey box with the white star circled item below for guidance. This grey box with the white star that says "Welcome" underneath it – this is the beginnings of your custom tab, and when users click it, where it leads to will become your custom page.

IMPORTANT LEARNING TIP: In the diagram above, also note the little drop down arrow immediately to the right of the circled grey star box. Whenever you click that down arrow, that puts you in editing mode for your custom tabs and associated pages.

G. The next step then is to customize this grey box with the white star and to get started making your custom tab page (the page to where clicking on the custom tab will lead you):

G.1   Click the drop down arrow to the right of the grey star box to get into editing mode.

G.2   After you click the down arrow (to the right of the star box), roll your cursor over the grey star box, and a little pencil appears in the upper right corner. Click on the pencil in the upper right corner of the grey star box.

G.3   From the drop down menu that results, choose edit settings, as shown below:

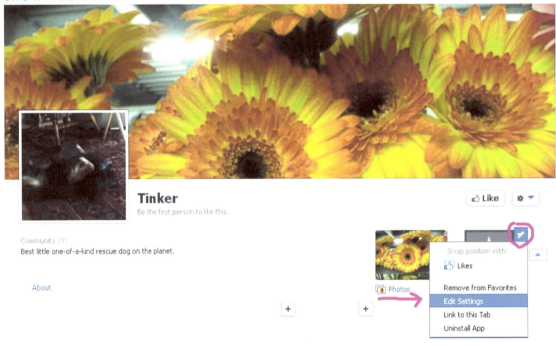

G.4   Now you will get a ittle box on your screen that lets you change the box name from "Welcome" (the default) to whatever you want. Some people use "START HERE" so people know to click on that box asap when they get to your fan page, some people keep welcome, some people use a teaser, it's up to you. For my TinkertheThinker page, I chose to call my custom tab "Buried Bones." You can also at the same time upload an image to replace that white star on the grey background. You need to make sure the image you upload is precisely 111 pixels wide by 74 pixels tall. You can use Adobe Photoshop to resize your image. When your done, return to the screen that has the editing box and click OK to save your changes.

G. 5   Now you will see your fan page screen again, and now the white star box has been transformed to your custom boc. You can see what I did below. Click on that newly transformed box, and you will be able to edit the actual contents of that custom page:

Click on your new customized box to edit the contents of the box

G.6 When you click in the center of your new box, you will get the following screen:

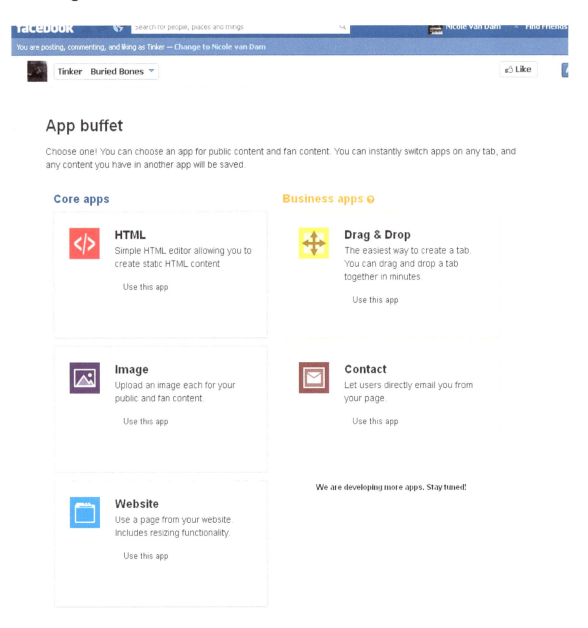

G.7   You can play with these, and if you choose the top left one that says "HTML" you can make some really cool custom html fan pages, but if you have already invested in a regular website there is no need to recreate the wheel: Here is the easiest, done in a minute, solution: Click on the lower left corner box that says "Website". The next screen will give you a place to fill in your URL of the website you already have. I typed in the website for my gardening blog, as follows: http://our1earth.com   (make sure you have the http:// at the beginning of whatever URL you type). See below for guidance:

Click Save & Publish and you are ... DONE!

Go test it out – go to your main Facebook business/fan page, then click on your new custom tab box and see where it leads you! You will see, framed in Facebook menus, the website for whatever URL you typed in! It's that SIMPLE! You cam simply incorporate any website URL you desire from your main site, with all its links and bells and whistles, into your Facebook business page in one easy step!

15

Step 4:

How to re-enter editing mode: If you wish to change the URL you incorporated into your custom tab (or if you used the HTML option instead of the website option to create your custom tab), you can re-enter the custom tab editing mode at any time by:

1. Clicking on the down arrow by your new box, to make sure you are in editing mode;
2. Clicking on your new box to bring you to the editing screen
3. Clicking on the 'admin tools' box in the resulting upper left corner
4. Clicking on the resulting green"Edit tab" box on the upper right side
5. Change the URL/do your html editing!

FANGATE: If you look at the image above, it also shows you how to incorporate "Fangate" which lets you show different content to those who have liked your page. This encourages folks to like your page to see the extra content. If you click on the Fangate tab as shown above, you will see: reen:

Click on the "Enable fangate" box to enable fangate.

Once you click the "Enable fangate" box, you will see the following screen:

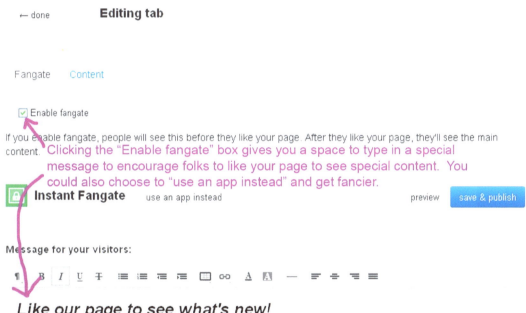

In the above screen you can either type in a simple message to encourage others to "like" you fan page to see special content, and Facebook will autocreate the page for you (with a red arrow directing people to like your page), or you can choose to use another app to make your own page for folks who have not yet liked your page . More specifically, if you choose to "use anotehr app" you will be directed to the same "App buffet" choices you had before – see below:

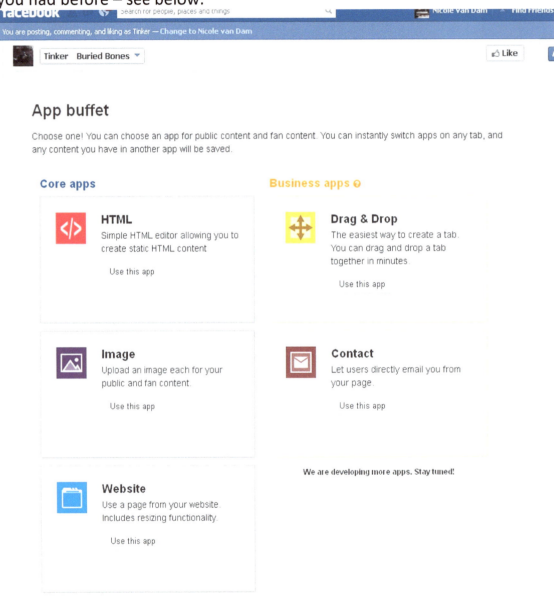

As before, at this "App buffet" you can choose "Website" (bottom left corner of the prior screen capture) to simply include a different URL, or you can choose "HTML" (above left of the preceding screen capture) to make your own special HTML message to encourage other sto like your page).

Some thoughts on Fangate: You have to decide what your goal is – my goal is not to have the most likes – my goal is to direct people to hopefully buy my books, so the fewer steps to that the better. For this reason, for the Tinker fan page that I created for this book, I chose to use fangate to make a page that encourages likes but also provides hyperlinks to http://SuperQuick.bz and to http://OnceUponaTime.bz (my children's books site). What I typed in was:

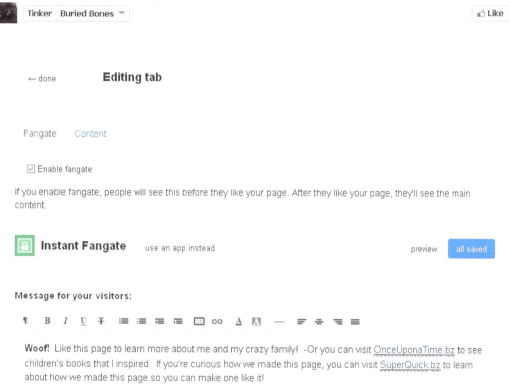

Please come visit http://www.facebook.com/tinkerthethinker and see what the custom "Start Here" tab looks like before you like this page, and then like the page and see what you get!

You can also incorporate Google analytics (if you have a Google analytics account) by:
1. Clicking on the down arrow by your new box, to make sure you are in editing mode;
2. Clicking on your new box to bring you to the editing screen
3. Clikcing on the 'admin tools' box in the resulting upper left corner
4. Clicking on the resulting settings box
5. Clicking on the "Google Analytics" choice and filling in the info requested.

Reordering custom tabs on your Fan/Business page: At some point, you might have more than one custom tab on your fan page. If you do, you might wish to reorder them. Facebook designed it so the photos tab always is first, but after that, you can reorder your tabs however you wish. Just click the down arrow next to your new box to put you in edit mode, then scroll over the box you wish to move, then click on the little pencil that results, then choose the "swap" option and put your new box in the place you choose in the tab order.

Remember to Manage Permissions: Another mission critical thing is to manage permissions. If you want to limit who can post on your page, you need to go to:

1. Click on "Edit Page" drop down menu at the top of your Admin panel for your fan page, and from that drop down menu select "Edit Settings"
2. Choose "Manage Permissions" on the resulting screen
3. Check (or uncheck) boxes to suit your preferences. Following is what I choose:

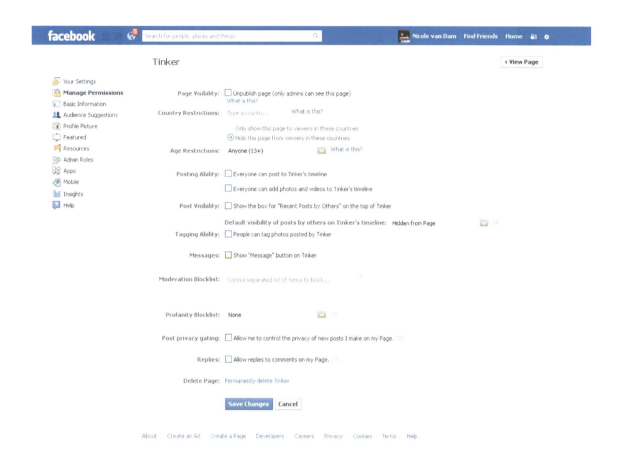

Make sure you click the blue save changes box above before you exit the page!

<mark>If you ever can't find your Facebook fan/business pages</mark>, login into Facebook to your personal page, click home, then along the left margin you will see the PAGES heading and your pages will be there.

21

Step 5: Advertising with Facebook

Facebook has a tremendous database (over 500 Million users – and counting!), and this database is tailored so that you can target your ads to exactly your demographic.

If you think your demographic is Cornell graduates who have dogs, you can choose to have your ad displayed to just those people! Facebook advertising is that powerful and easy to target!

That's why this effort is worth doing.

What is a Facebook ad? A Facebook ad is a little photo and a few words that from time to time appear on Facebook users profile pages, and if you see one on your profile page, usually that ad will be about something you have expressed an interest in when you made your profile.   For example, I like Bill Bryson, and I have seen Bill Bryson book ads pop up on my Facebook page.

The way a Facebook ad works, is that Facebook sends a small box with a photo and a few words to the Facebook pages of those people who you choose, up to the amount of your ad campaign budget. If someone sees your ad and clicks it (in the pay-per-click model, which is what I use and suggest), then that person is sent to a link you choose.

The next step then is to create a Facebook ad:

22

To create a Facebook ad, click on "Build Audience" from the upper Ademin Panel menu bar, then from the resulting drop down menu, choose "Create an Ad" – see below for guidance:

Next you will see a page entitled "Advertise on Facebook" and you will have some decisions to make:

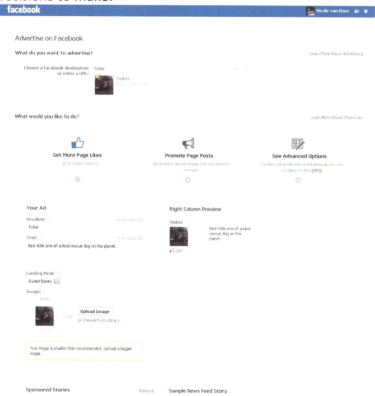

<mark>First, you can link your advertisement to anything</mark> – an Amazon page that is selling your book for example! In other words, just because you got to the Facebook advertising section via the fan page you just created, that does not mean that you have to have your ad linked to that fan page. Remember, the fewer clicks between the Facebook ad and 'the call to action' (what you want your customer to do), the better.

DETAIL: To enter a URL different from your facebook page, click the x by the box that shows your Facebook page and you will get the following menu:

-So, the first decision you need to make is what URL to link the ad to. Again, if I'm selling a book, I link it either the Amazon page for the book or my website page that has the Amazon link clearly marked. You want this to be easy for someone who doesn't know their way around your site/Facebook pages.

Let's say you enter in an external URL.
Once you submit that external URL to Facebook, Facebook actually tries to make life easy for you, by trying to autogenerate/create an ad for you to get you started.
It will take photos of your site and wording off your site, and it usually does a good but not perfect job, so you will have to perfect things a little. All you need to do to get an ad on Facebook is literally to fill in the information they request, and it takes 30 minutes perhaps the first time, and only a few minutes after that!

It is up to you how you want to clean up your ad, but the next step is to do that. You can change the wording that Facebook guessed was right, and you can change the image they guessed for you as well. Fyi, I never show social activity next to my ad.

Targeting your Ad: Next is the fun part. You need to target who you want to see your ad. I suggest you try a few different ads targeted at different people, this will help you learn about your target demographic (fancy marketing way to say your typical customer). Where do they live? Where did they go to school? What hobbies do they have? For example, if I were advertising a gardening book and recipes based on my climate, I would target folks in CA and maybe Oregon and Carolina whose precise interests include gardening, organic, cooking, etc. If I

25

were advertising my children's book about my Leonberger dog, I would choose very differently – now the whole world who speaks English who has a child and a Leonberger would be my target market. It's not that others won't like the book too – it's just that I only want to pay for ads to my best bet!

Look at how you can tailor your marketing efforts precisiely

to your **demographic –**

This makes Facebook a marketer's dream!

A very good thing about Facebook ads is that it helps you define and understand who your typical/most likely customer might be. It also helps you with precision target those customers, and test your theories on marketing.

Next you set your campaign budget. Now the money part comes in. Advertising on Facebook is not free.
You can pay per click up to a daily budget or up to a lifetime budget. You can pause or eliminate ads, have one or more ads on an ad campaign, and more than one campaign running per time. You can offer to pay less per click than their suggested amount. Paying less can still work.

By way of example, I usually go $1 per day and bid 15-25 cents per click. I don't care what the suggested bid says, I stay firm to that price range. That's it!!! That way I know I won't be spending more than $30 per month advertising my book. Each month I can compare sales to what I spent advertising – and if an ad doesn't pay for itself I can halt the ad, maybe change it, maybe choose to advertise something else, maybe take a break. If you are an Amazon affiliate, make sure you always use the Amazon affiliate link version to direct folks to Amazon because then you get an Amazon Affiliate commission as well as the royalty for the sale of your book.

TIPS:

Before you place your ad order you can review it
again and see the tailored demographic.

**Remember to make sure your landing page is really nice
and has all the links and information it needs to have
before you advertise it, otherwise you are wasting your money.**

To change what you pay per click, to change your daily or lifetime budget, to revise your ads, create new ads, or pause or eliminate ads, all you need to do is click on the blue box that says "Ads Manager" on any of your pages.

Step 6: Adobe Photoshop Primer

To create my ads and website images, I use Adobe Photoshop, one of the tools of the trade I recommend. I work with both version CS-5 (a recent version) and an oooold CS-3 version – the CS version works GREAT if you have an older computer. The screen captures below are from the CS-3 version – but I just compared them for you and the top menu choices are identical (except that CS-5 version of Photoshop has a 3D menu choice, not needed to create your ads or website art). In other words, the following screen captures should work very well to guide you in CS-5 as well.

A. Detail on how to start a new document in Adobe Photoshop:

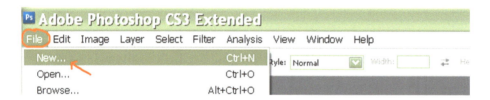

NOTE: To save your Photoshop document as you work on it, select File and then select Save. You should do this often!

Now to start: Choose File from the upper menu, and from the resulting drop down menu choose New. This generates the following dialogue box. You will need to use the drop down menus inside the dialogue box to change pixels to inches. You will put your cursor in the dialogue box and type in the exact width and height that you need for your particular purpose.

28

B. Designing in Photoshop

Once you put in the dimensions and resolution per step A above, a new blank document opens, and your scree will look something like this – you have a blank canvas waiting for your creativity:

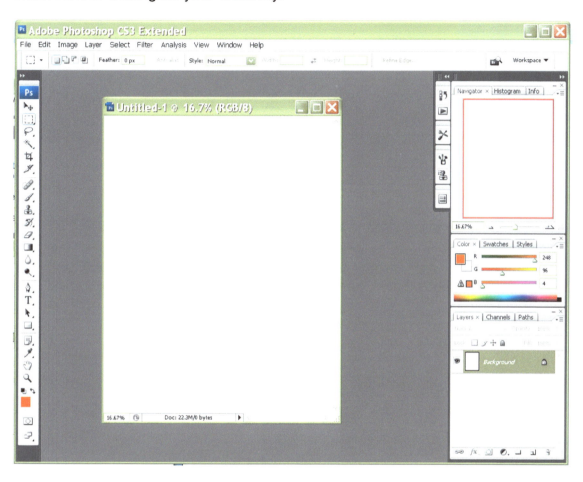

Let's assume that you don't have an image to use, so that your image will be made of color and words (the title of your book) only. The reality is, big contrast and color sells, so you need to think BOLD for your image to pop.

The next step is to choose a background color – let's use a dark color like navy blue:

Click here to pick a color

16.67%   Doc: 22.3M/0 bytes

When you click the colored box as above, you get a pop-up that is the fabulous Adobe Photoshop color selector box, and you then choose the color family from the rainbow colored bar. Because we want a blue background, click on the blue color of the rainbow bar. See the arrow in the screen capture that follows:

When you click blue on the rainbow color bar as shown above, then you get the following screen capture, that gives you all sorts of blue shades to choose from. Click the shade of blue you want for your color background. I circled in orange where I clicked my mouse.

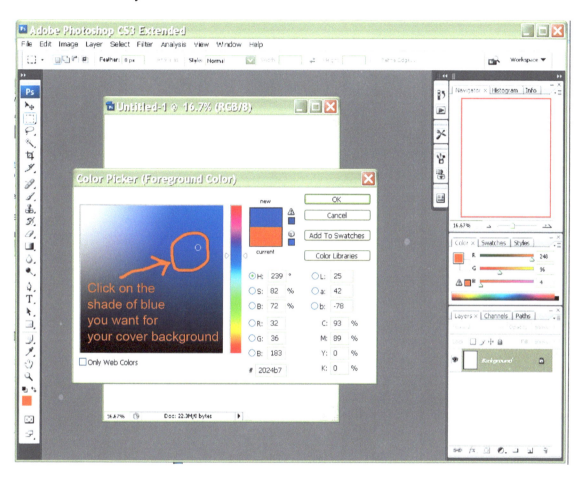

Here is what you will see next, and the following screen capture also shows where you need to click next:

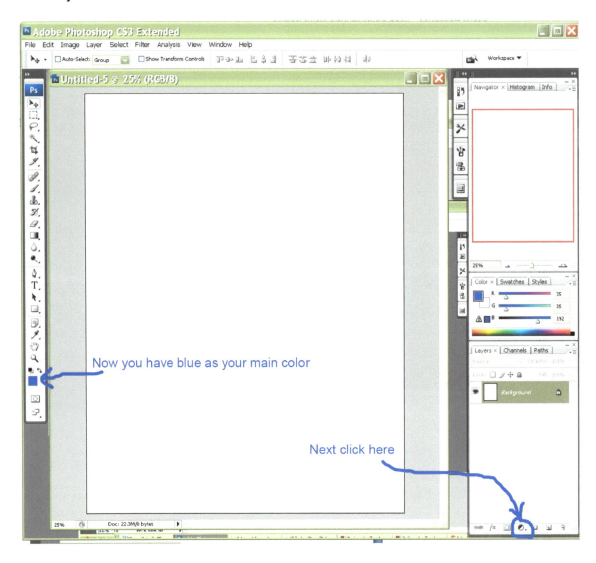

When you click that little circle shown above, you will get a drop down menu – choose "Solid Color" from that drop down menu.

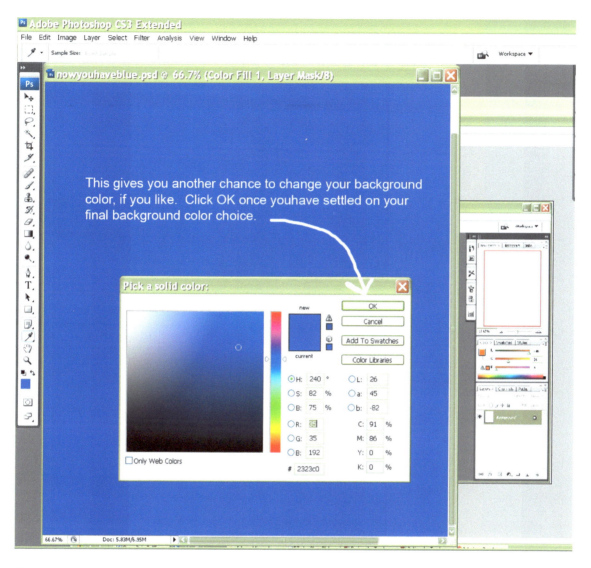

Once you click OK, you will have a document that now has a solid blue background.

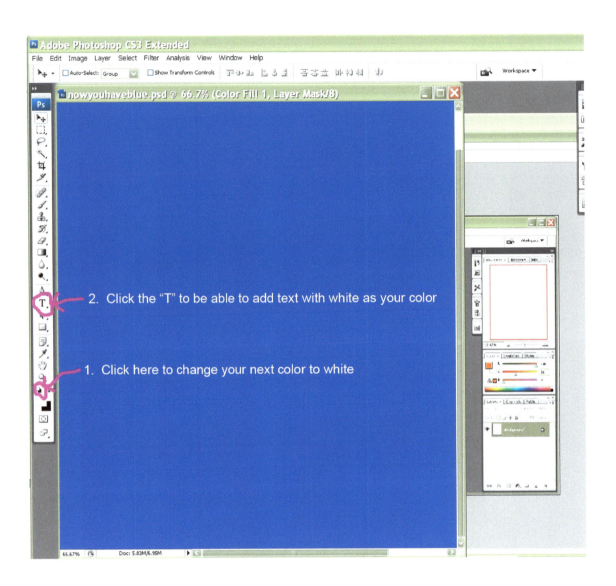

2. Click the "T" to be able to add text with white as your color

1. Click here to change your next color to white

Click with your cursor where in the blue cover you want to start typing your title. You can change the font style, color, and size easily using the top bar as shown below. Experiment till you like it!

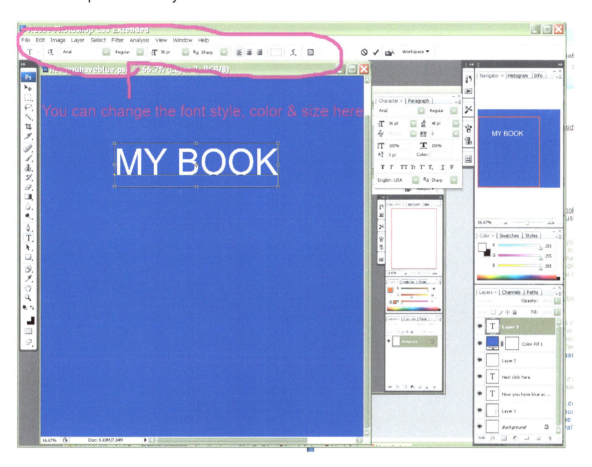

Of course, you might want to move your text. You will also wish to add another line of text, in a different color and size. Following is a screen capture showing how to do that.

To move text, as shown below, you will click on the top left icon in the tool bar as shown in the following screen capture.

To add more text, first click the top left icon in the tool bar, then click the "T" in the tool bar. Click with your mouse wherever in the background you want to start typing your new text, and type it in. (Remember, you can use the top toolbar to change the font size, style and color, as previously shown in the image above).

35

Once you have added text for a second time, look at the lower right "layer" box (see the screen capture below). Each time you typed in new text, you created a new "layer." You will see by look at the "layer" box in the bottom right corner that the dark blue background has its own layer in the layer box too. This is important, because you can only make changes to the "active" layer – the active layer is the layer in the layer box that looks a little darker that the others (highlighted, so to speak). When you want to work on a different layer, all you need to do is click on that layer – very easy! So when you want to switch between text layers, all you need to do is click on the "T" of the text layer that you want to work on. If you double click the "T", the entire text gets highlighted. If you screw up a layer, all you need to do is click the "eye" icon by that layer in the lower right layer box, and that layer becomes invisible – it's still there, but it won't print or be seen. If you want the layer to be visible again, just click its eye icon again.

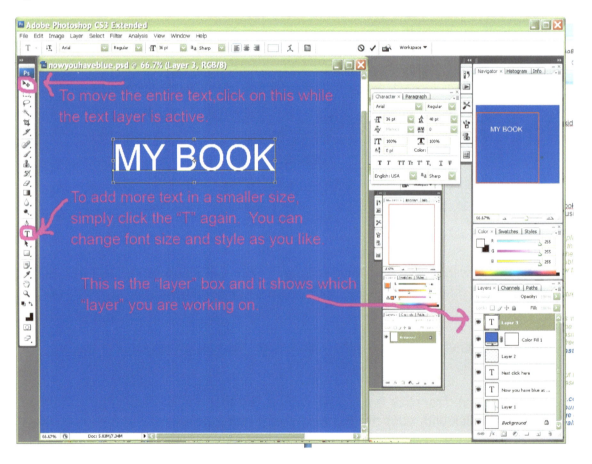

Once you have typed in your two pieces of text – your title and your name as the author, it is time to pretty it up a bit. If you don't have a picture to use, a simple colorful box can do the trick. Here is a screen capture showing how to do that in easily:

Step 1 is that you click the box on the toolbar, as shown below.

Step 2 is that you click on the top bar (where it says "Style" and that gives you a drop down menu as shown below. Click on the box in the drop down menu as shown below. By doing this you have chosen to make an outline box of the color shown in the top menu. In the picture below, that color is pink. I am going to change it to bright yellow by clicking on the pink box in the top menu, which will give me the color picker again.

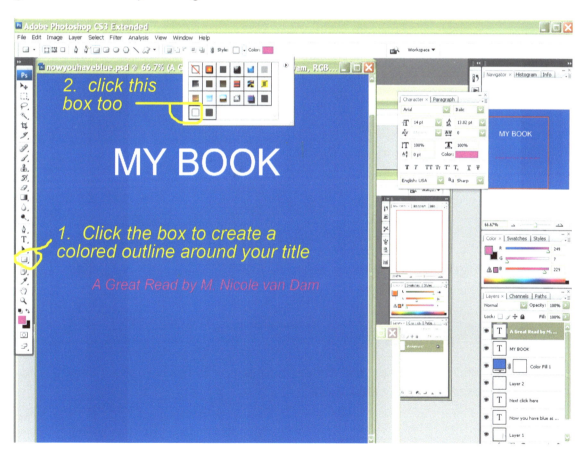

The outline of your box might look too thin. To experiment with outline thicknesses, you can click on the word "Stroke" in the layer box for that layer you are working on. See the screen capture below for an example:

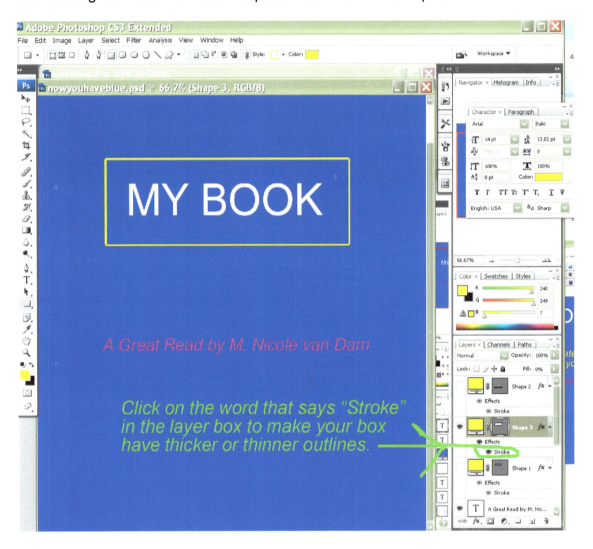

Next, let's repeat the process and make another box to really make it pop. —And a few more boxes! But why stop there?

Photoshop comes preloaded with patterns – let's access some of those. Here's how:

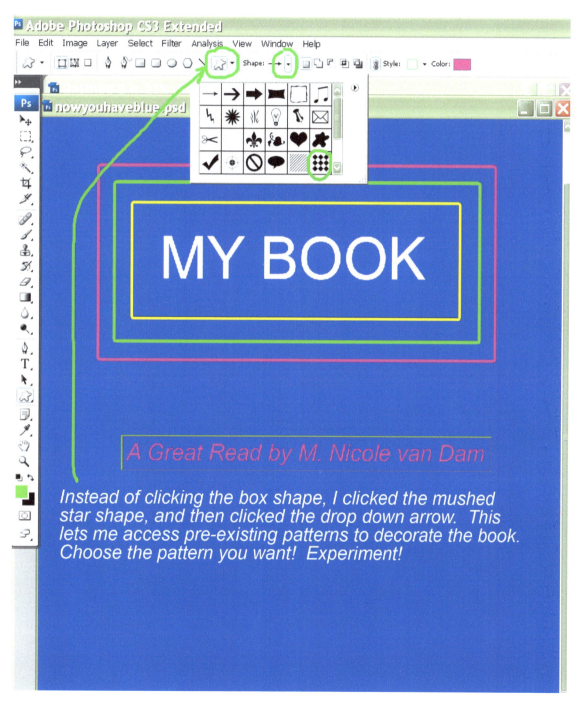

Instead of clicking the box shape, I clicked the mushed star shape, and then clicked the drop down arrow. This lets me access pre-existing patterns to decorate the book. Choose the pattern you want! Experiment!

As shown above, in the upper tool bar, choose the squiggly star shape, then choose shape to pick a pre-existing patten, and now choose where you want to place your pattern and drag your mouse to get the right size. For the cover below, I chose the lightbulb pattern, with an orange outline and yellow fill. I dren it quite large. Then I selected the T layer in the layer box (lower right corner of your workspace) and I chose the text with my name in it, and moved that down. The end result is a catchy cover, using nothing but Photoshop!

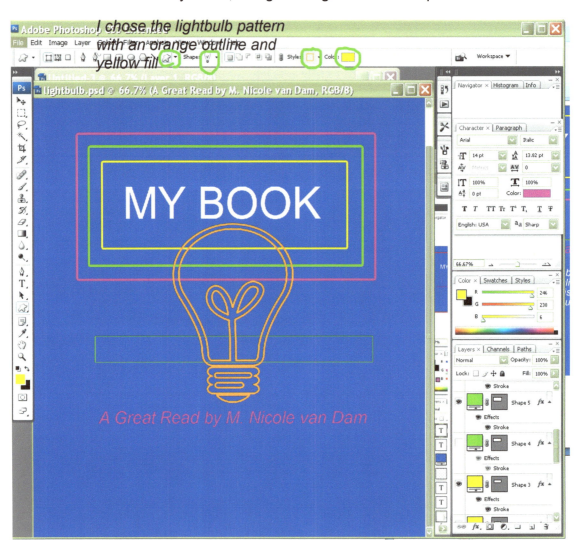

If you had an image/phot that you want to use (and have the legal right to use), then to insert that image into your cover simply choose File then Place and when you click place you will be given the opportunity to browse to your image. See below:

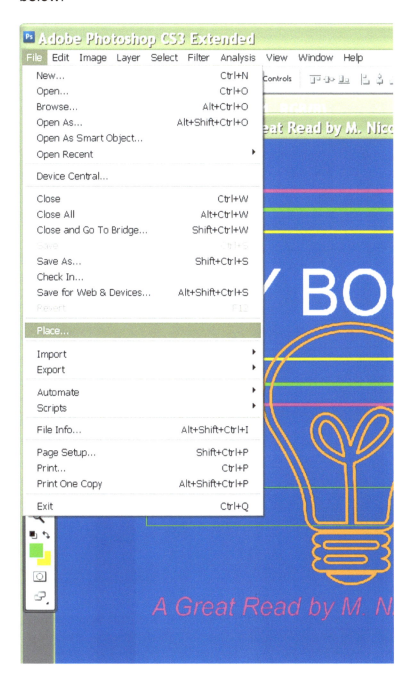

After you browse to your image and select it, it will appear on your cover, but it will undoubtedly be the wrong size and not where you want it. First click the arrow key in the upper left of your toolbox (see below), and then when the popup box appears choose "Place" see below). Now you can move the image around on your cover. To change the image size, hold the shift key while dragging any corner of your image to make it the right size. See the screen capture below for details:

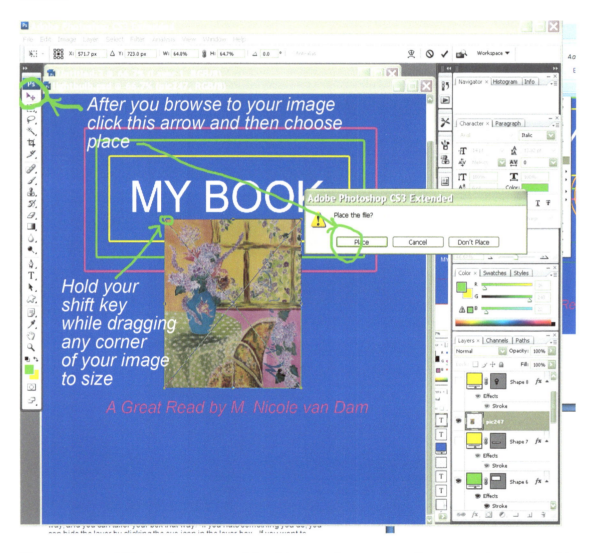

The powers of Photoshop, even this older version, are endless – and you should play with it! You will discover there are more than one way to do things, and you will find the way that is most comfortable for you. However, now you know the basic parts of the Photoshop screen, and here they are, plus some extra pointers:

PHOTOSHOP POINTERS"

- The toolbox default location is on the left side of your Photoshop screen
- The layer box default location is on the right side of your Photoshop screen
- When you select a tool from the toolbox, your Photoshop workspace changes - you will usually see a menu specifically for the tool you selected above your Photoshop document, and that tool specific menu lets you tailor that tool – you can tailor fonts that way, and you can tailor the pink and yellow and green boxes shown in my sample cover that way.
- If you hate something you do, you can hide the layer by clicking the eye icon in the layer box.
- If one thing you drew in Photoshop covers up something behind it, then in Photoshop terms, you want to move the one layer so that it is on top of the other layer, instead of behind it. To do this, all you need to do is click on the layer in the layer box that you want to be on top of the other, and holding your mouse down drag the lower layer up in the layer box so that the layer you are dragging shows up in the layer box above the layer that was blocking it. In other words, working in the layer box on the right side of your screen, you simply drag the layer to where you want it to be.
- If you want to permanently delete a layer, simply right click on the layer you want to delete and then choose "delete layer."
- If you want to add a layer, choose "Layer" from the upper menu bar of the Photoshop screen and then choose "New" from the drop down menu, and then choose Layer.
- One fun and easy thing to do in Photoshop is to play with the opacity of a layer. Click on a layer, and then at the top of your layer box, click "opacity" and then slide the slider under opacity to less than 100%. This makes that specific layer transparent – pretty fun!
- To resize a layer, click that layer in the layer box, then click Edit from the top menu bar of the Photoshop workspace, then click "Transform" then click scale. Drag the corners as desired. If you hold down the shift key while you drag the corners, the item you are resizing will scale up or down proportionately.
- Play, play, play! Photoshop is amazing!
- Remember to save frequently!!!

Thoughts to Ponder & Recommendations:

I highly recommend, if you have not done so already, that you take a class on Adobe Photoshop and basic HTML coding so that you can make your Facebook and other web endeavors as beautiful and painless as possible. If you really wish to be brave, learn Java scripting also!

About the Author

M. Nicole van Dam, in addition to exploring entrepreneurship and innovation, is an internationally licensed artist working in many media, such as oils, acrylics, water color, pastels, pen and ink, and silk. In each work, one can find a passionate celebration of nature's beauty and diversity, which is Nicole's primary inspiration.

Nicole, a California native born of Dutch immigrant parents, was educated on the East Coast and is now living by California's Central Coast with her much-loved husband, dogs and birds. Nicole writes about her artistic endeavors, pets and vegetable garden at her news blog, Wishes.bz.

Nicole is also an internationally published poet and author of adult and children's books. An example of a children's book that she wrote and illustrated is "Inca Dink, the Great Houndini" (please see www.IncaDink.com to learn more). She also authored "Tempo –The Rhythm and Rhyme of the Artist" – a fun and inspirational book for adults blending art, poetry and philosophy.

Dedication

This Book is Dedicated to my wonderful parents and to my patient husband, Jay, who supports me in all I do.

OTHER BOOKS BY M. NICOLE VAN DAM

SuperQuick ® Self-Publishing: On Demand Publishing & eBooks Made Easy

SuperQuick ® Savvy Business Thinking Points & Interviews

SuperQuick ® Facebook – Easy and Fast Pages & Ads

SuperQuick® Wordpress – Easy, FREE and Fast Website, Smart Phone and e-Commerce Solutions!

SuperQuick® Solutions – Web Essentials: Time and Money Saving Tips for Website, Social Media and e-Commerce

Exploring the Successful You: A Guided Tour

Tempo – The Rhythm and Rhyme of the Artist

M. Nicole van Dam, a Retrospective 2010

Inca Dink, The Great Houndini

Rosie and Emma Plant a Seed

This Little Puppy

The Background Story of Inca Dink, The Great Houndini

To learn more, please visit *Nicole.bz*

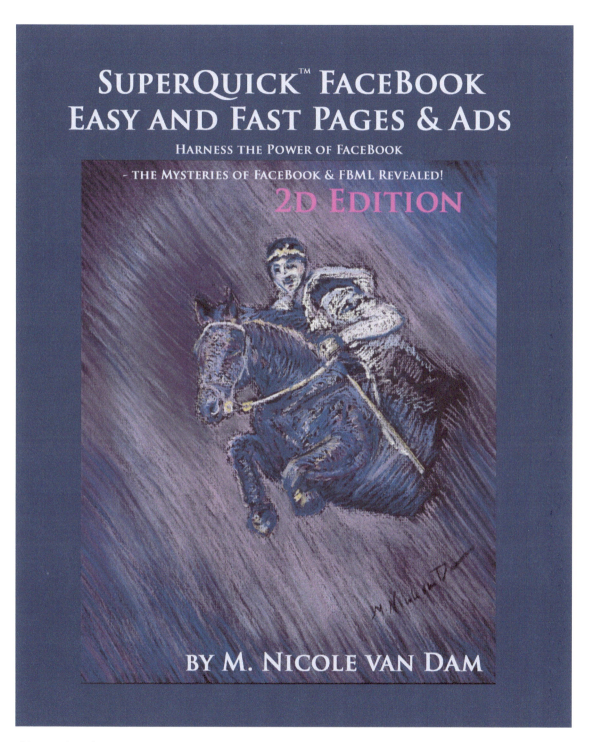

About the Cover Art: "Leap of Faith™" is artwork by M. Nicole van Dam.

Gondolier of Venice ™

    An example of an internationally licensed painting by M. Nicole van Dam.

All artwork used under license and © and ™ M. Nicole van Dam. Learn more about this art at Nicole.bz

www.ingramcontent.com/pod-product-compliance
Lightning Source LLC
Chambersburg PA
CBHW050937060326
40689CB00040B/635

* 9 7 8 0 6 1 5 4 5 1 4 9 7 *